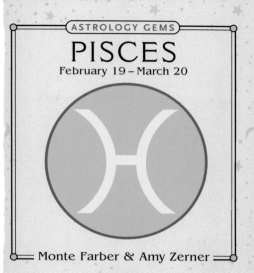

ASTROLOGY GEMS

PISCES
February 19 – March 20

Monte Farber & Amy Zerner

Sterling Publishing Co., Inc.
New York

Text © 2006 by Monte Farber
Art © 2006 by Amy Zerner

10 9 8 7 6 5 4 3

Published by Sterling Publishing Co., Inc.
387 Park Avenue South, New York, NY 10016

Distributed in Canada by Sterling Publishing
c/o Canadian Manda Group, 165 Dufferin Street
Toronto, Ontario, Canada M6K 3H6

Distributed in the United Kingdom by GMC
Distribution Services
Castle Place, 166 High Street, Lewes, East Sussex,
England BN7 1XU

Distributed in Australia by Capricorn Link (Australia)
Pty. Ltd.
P.O. Box 704, Windsor, NSW 2756, Australia

Printed in China

Sterling ISBN-13: 978-1-4027-4182-1
        ISBN-10: 1-4027-4182-0

For information about custom editions, special sales,
premium and corporate purchases, please contact
Sterling Special Sales Department at 800-805-5489 or
specialsales@sterlingpub.com.

What's Your Sign?

When someone asks you "What's your sign?" you know what that person really means is "What's your astrological sign?" Professional astrologers more often use the phrase "Sun sign," a term reflecting the concept that a person's sign is determined by which of the twelve signs of the zodiac the Sun appeared to be passing through at the moment she was born. The zodiac is the narrow band of sky circling the Earth's equator through which the Sun, the Moon, and the planets appear to move when viewed by us here on Earth.

Astrology's Gift

Astrology, which has been around for thousands of years, is the study of how planetary positions relate to earthly events and people. Its long and rich history has resulted in a wealth of philosophical and psychological wisdom, the basic concepts of which we are going to share with you in the pages of this book. As the Greek philosopher Heracleitus (c. 540–c. 480 BCE) said, "Character is destiny." Who you are—complete with all of your goals, tendencies, habits, virtues, and vices—will

determine how you act and react, thereby creating your life's destiny. Like astrology itself, our Astrology Gems series is designed to help you to better know yourself and those you care about. You will then be better able to use your free will to shape your life to your liking.

Does Astrology Work?

Many people rightly question how astrology can divide humanity into twelve Sun signs and make predictions that can be correct for everyone of the same sign. The simple answer is that it cannot do that—that's newspaper astrology, entertaining but not the real thing. Rather, astrology can help you understand your strengths and weaknesses so that you can better accept yourself as you are and use your strengths to compensate for your weaknesses. Real astrology is designed to help you to become yourself fully.

Remember, virtually all the music in the history of Western music has been composed using variations of the same twelve notes. Similarly, the twelve Sun signs of astrology are basic themes rich with meaning that each of us expresses differently to create and respond to the unique opportunities and challenges of our life.

PISCES

February 19–March 20

Planet
Neptune

Element
Water

Quality
Mutable

Day
Thursday

Season
winter

Colors
lavender, sea green, aqua

Plants
wisteria, gardenia, lotus

Perfume
ylang-ylang

Gemstones
aquamarine, coral,
mother-of-pearl, pearl

Metal
tin

Personal qualities
Empathetic, artistic, compassionate,
selfless, and psychically attuned

We call the following words "keywords" because they can help you unlock the core meaning of the astrological sign of Pisces. Each keyword represents issues and ideas that are of supreme importance and prominence in the lives of people born with Pisces as their Sun sign. You will usually find that every Pisces embodies at least one of these keywords in the way he makes a living:

sensitivity • spiritualism

moodiness • otherworldliness

suffering in silence • vagueness

inspiration • faith • idealism

alternative medicine • fantasy

receptivity • imagination • dreams

martyrdom • confusion • illusion

sacrifice • surrender • escape

drug addiction and alcoholism

spirit guides • intuition • ESP

mind-body-spirit connection

Pisces' Symbolic Meaning

Pisces is the last sign of the zodiac. Because it is the last of the twelve signs, it contains a bit of all of them. If they take the time and investigate a little, people born under this sign often realize that they are literally picking up on the feelings of others. This explains why Pisces people are so easily able to understand how other people are feeling.

In fact, Pisceans are so sensitive to the feelings of others that it is not good for them to be near people who are angry, sad, or disturbed. If they are in conflict with themselves as the Piscean symbol suggests—two fish locked in tension, forever pulling each other in opposite directions—one side of this conflict can represent the personality whose inner self is always preparing to retreat from the world.

Pisces is associated with both empathy and telepathy. This natural ability to be invisibly connected to those around them and those around the world is both the blessing and the curse of all

Pisceans. It enables them to feel exactly how to help those they care about, which is a Piscean specialty, but it is exhausting and hard on a Piscean person's emotions to have other people's lives intrude so on their own.

Pisces is one of the four Mutable Sun signs in astrology (the other three are Gemini, Virgo, and Sagittarius). Mutable signs are able to adapt and adjust. Pisces is also one of the three Water Sun signs in the zodiac (the other two are Scorpio and Cancer). Water signs value their emotions and their intuition.

When they turn their sensitivity to the real world, Pisceans have the capacity to make incredible amounts of money in business ventures. If you think that seems unlikely given Pisces' reputation for dreaminess and escapism, remember that as the last sign, Pisces contains a bit of all the other ones. Pisceans are most aware of both the things that unite us all and the immense differences between people. This is one of their great strengths, but if they let themselves be totally ruled by their emotions or let the sorrow of the human condition push them to escapist behavior, it can turn into a great weakness. When they learn to balance their innate intuitive skills with a logical approach that does not ignore what is real but unpleasant, they can accomplish great things.

Recognizing a Pisces

Pisces people have an air of mystery. Their eyes are very sensitive and caring, and they typically have a warm smile and the quality of empathy. There is a quietness in their manner. They are approachable, as though they truly understand human sorrows and failings. Although they may appear slender or have delicate features, they possess an inner strength that seems to radiate from the soul.

Pisces' Typical Behavior and Personality Traits

❁ has a warm, sympathetic heart

❁ very romantic

❁ rarely jealous, but gets hurt all the same

❁ often appears vague and dreamy

❁ protects her emotional vulnerability

❁ talks slowly and is knowledgeable on many subjects

❁ subtle while appearing to be helpless or incapable

- organized; manages the finances extremely well

- has few prejudices

- emotionally involved

- not ambitious for status, fame, or fortune

- cannot easily be fooled

- has few material needs, but needs her dreams

- does not try to dominate her partner in any way

- needs to belong to someone

What Makes a Pisces Tick?

The lesson for Pisces centers on why her life does not provide her with as many opportunities as she would like to use her unique sensitivity to others to gain the appreciation of those she would most like to help and associate with. People born under the sign Pisces want to learn how to get close enough to people to be of assistance to them without becoming overwhelmed by their needs and neediness. The more honest and honorable a Piscean is, the more she hesitates. Pisceans seem to fear that the world will expect more of them than they can give.

The Pisces Personality Expressed Positively

A Pisces who is empowered by the best characteristics of the sign is a source of help and inspiration both to himself and to others. The sensitivity of Pisceans is most useful when those born under this sign have a good sense of self and a lot of confidence. When they do, they are wonderful people to be around—full of joy, inspiration, and profound intuition.

On a Positive Note

Pisceans displaying the positive characteristics associated with their sign also tend to be:

- shy, gentle, and kind
- trusting and hospitable
- understanding of others
- romantic
- loving and caring
- mystical
- creative
- helpful to anyone in distress
- compassionate

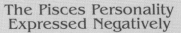

The Pisces Personality Expressed Negatively

Pisceans who are unable to separate themselves from the drama and unhappiness in other people's lives display the negative characteristics of their sign. They often feel dragged down by problems around them yet are frustrated by their inability to do anything to make them better. Disappointed Pisceans may seek escape through drugs or alcohol, the effects of which make them more powerless.

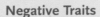

Negative Traits

Pisceans displaying the negative character-istics associated with their sign also tend to be:

- dependent

- escapist, potentially losing touch with reality

- depressive and self-pitying

- temperamental

- gullible and liable to give their all in a lost cause

- prone to blaming themselves

- too emotionally involved with the problems of others

Ask a Pisces If...

Ask a Pisces if you want to know the meaning of life. The Piscean is unlikely to put it in terms as broad as this, but he will, by some small act or utterance, help you to understand that it is through compassion, caring, and a spirit that is open to receive the love of others that true happiness exists. Pisceans are plugged in to the universe in a way that is otherworldly.

Pisces As Friends

Pisces are humorous and caring friends, even if there are long periods of time between get-togethers. In general, Pisces like friends who are useful and reassuring. In return, they give unprejudiced understanding and loyalty to their friends. Pisces are emotionally attached to their friends and rarely take notice if a friend is taking advantage of this involvement. Pisces can be a confusing person, so arrangements to meet with friends may be difficult to make.

Pisceans always think up something interesting to do and enjoy any kind of artistic venture. They can sometimes seem cool and offhand. This is usually temporary and due to a moment of insecurity. Pisces does not find it easy to conform; friends with conservative attitudes may find this a difficulty.

Looking for Love

The element of sacrifice does not fit easily with the standard view of courtship and romance. The exception to this occurs when a Pisces meets someone through her dedication to helping others. If both partners are on the helping end, this relationship would be more prone to lasting than if one partner was helping the other person. This would not be a relationship founded on mutual support, so it might need substantial reworking if the person receiving help no longer needed it. Sometimes, relationships last only as long as the problems being worked on exist.

If a Pisces does not have a relationship, the problem may be caused by his trying to escape reality in some way. Any dependence on drinking, drugs, cults, or even traditional religion will prevent him from being himself and seeing people for who they really are. Pisces should never give up his own beliefs and identity in a relationship where to get or keep his partner he has to deceive her, or himself.

The Piscean quest for romance is rooted in fantasy as much as reality. For other signs, this can be a mistake. But Pisces needs the illusion to keep the reality of love alive. If there is no fantasy, Pisces cannot fall in love in the first place. As long as Pisces' partner understands that it is up to her to help support the fantasy and, occasionally, make it come true, this way of looking at love works for Pisceans.

Finding That Special Someone

If a Pisces works in an artistic atmosphere, she will most certainly find a love interest there, or at a cultural happening. Otherwise, being involved in charitable causes will put Pisceans into contact with people who share their need to do good things for others.

First Dates

Pisceans enjoy the hearts-and-flowers routine, but only if it is sincere and not just an attempt to flatter their ego. Pisceans are more traditional than they realize. They take pleasure in simple dates like dinner and a movie or just a stroll while holding hands. They are not impressed by fancy surroundings or decor, and are as likely to enjoy a midnight burger at an all-night diner as a gourmet meal at one of the city's best eateries. Pisces believes that it is the company, not the surroundings, that makes the date special.

Pisces in Love

To Pisces, there is no difference between love, affection, and romance. A Pisces is romantic, is eager to please, and adapts to the demands of the relationship. A Pisces who feels unloved is an unhappy person to whom life seems very gray. Love revitalizes Pisceans. They can sometimes appear to be delicate, helpless, or vulnerable, but being loved enables Pisceans to cope very well with a range of difficulties, problems, and tragedies and allows their spiritual nature to blossom.

Undying Love

A Pisces sometimes stays in a relationship even when he is being deceived or treated badly. He must face the problem and take immediate steps to correct it. Pisces may sometimes leave a relationship for no clear reason. If the partner will not do what is necessary, then Pisces should do everything he can to get out of the situation. Forgiveness can occur at a distance, too.

Pisces will often show much sympathetic understanding and will try to retain a friendly relationship with the one he has left.

Expectations in Love

Pisces is the most romantic sign of the zodiac. Once in love, Pisceans are very caring, sensitive, and ready to sacrifice their own happiness for the sake of those they love. However, all too often, denial is used as a way of avoiding reality. Many people would rather convince themselves that they are in a fine relationship rather than admit their problems. Even the most spiritual and powerful force in the universe, forgiveness, may be being used as a disguise for denial and weakness. If alcohol, drugs, abuse, violence, or adultery is standing between a Pisces and the truly loving relationship that she dreams of, these dangerous and destructive forces cannot be denied or condoned.

What Pisceans Look For

Most people say that they are more inter-
ested in what's "inside" than in a love
interest's appearance, but Pisceans really
mean it, though it is probably truer to say
that their love makes anyone beautiful or
handsome. Pisceans look for someone
whose life and spirit can be transformed
by their love. They may even fall in love
with a person who is very troubled, so
that they can act as their spiritual rescuer
or savior.

If Pisces Only Knew…

If Pisces only knew that they are capable of extraordinary strength and discipline, they would not worry about not measuring up to the challenges, both big and small, that come their way. At times, what they perceive to be a weakness is actually strength in the way that their great sensitivity allows them to deal with burdens that other, less-perceptive people cannot handle. Pisceans are accustomed to being treated by others as if they are emotionally fragile beings, and at times this causes them to have a less-than-stellar opinion of themselves, which is unfair.

Marriage

The married Pisces will bring great joy to the household with his wonderful imagination. Marriage gives male Pisces more self-assurance. The person who contemplates becoming the marriage partner of a typical Pisces must realize that Pisces will expect to be supported—emotionally or financially. Given this, the person who partners Pisces can expect loyalty and sensitive understanding in return.

Partners should be prepared to undertake the practical, administrative side of the marriage, leaving Piscean partners free to draw upon their artistic natures, and therefore exercise their creativity and understanding.

Pisces wants a marriage partner who supports and encourages her dreams in every respect. Pisces may sometimes appear to be a helpless, absentminded person, but once she feels secure in the relationship, she feels free to believe in the beauty and spiritual goodness of their partnership.

Pisces' Opposite Sign

Detail-conscious Virgo is Pisces' complementary sign. Like Pisces, Virgo is compassionate and eager to be of service, but is more disciplined and can help Pisces understand how best to shoulder her responsibilities in the world. Virgo can teach Pisces the value of self-discipline and how to become motivated. Pisces' gentleness has the power to make Virgo understand that sometimes criticism is just plain harping.

Pairing Up

In general, if people display the characteristics typical of their sign, intimate relationships between a Pisces and another individual can be described as follows:

Pisces with Pisces

Harmonious; a truly romantic pairing with incredibly soulful results

Pisces with Aries

Harmonious, though Aries will always want to take the lead

Pisces with Taurus

Harmonious, creating a good balance between passion and domesticity

Pisces with Gemini
Difficult, if Gemini can't appreciate Pisces' spiritual side

Pisces with Cancer
Harmonious; a happily-ever-after relationship

Pisces with Leo
Turbulent, yet with a karmic connection that just won't quit

Pisces with Virgo
Difficult, but the partners are supportive of each other's needs

Pisces with Libra
Turbulent, unless Pisces allows Libra to shine in the spotlight

Pisces with Scorpio
Harmonious; deeply spiritual and
incredibly passionate

Pisces with Sagittarius
Difficult; an emotional roller coaster,
but fun

Pisces with Capricorn
Harmonious, so long as Capricorn
learns to be tender

Pisces with Aquarius
Harmonious, since personality
differences can't spoil their love

If Things Don't Work Out

It can be very difficult for a Piscean to get out of an unhappy relationship. Even if there is no love left, Pisces is sure to continue to feel a sense of duty to his partner. It doesn't matter to Pisceans if there is clearly someone at fault in the breakup, because they will feel that it is at least partially their fault. Initially it isn't easy for them to move on after a breakup, but after a period that constitutes emotional mourning, they are ready to move forward with their life.

Pisces at Work

Pisceans can be very happy at work so long as they understand that they should not look to find all their contentment and satisfaction from doing a job. They don't always know that striking a balance is important in life, but they do notice it if there is something lacking in their existence as a result.

Even though Pisceans may be talented in their chosen field, it does not necessarily mean that the mantle of leadership comes easily to them. Actually, they may be uncomfortable with it, and so it can take a lot of talking by a person in authority whom they respect to make Pisceans realize their true potential. Pisceans may need to go through a period of adjustment as they grow in to their skills and leadership role.

There is a spiritual element to everything a Pisces dedicates his life to, and this can include work. When properly motivated, Pisceans can find great success as well as happiness resulting from their success. Once Pisces learns that being career oriented does not go hand-in-hand with materialism and greed, he is ready to welcome success as an option.

Typical Occupations

Because of their versatility, Pisces often follow several vocations during their lifetime. Working with large institutions such as the government, hospitals, the armed forces, major corporations, or charitable causes suits them. The intuitive and spiritual qualities of Pisceans can lead them into careers in religion and spirituality, or to service as mediums, mystics, and healers. Still others are creative cooks and chefs. They have a love of water and can be found in work that keeps them near the sea.

Pisces are sometimes better working by themselves than for someone else. Their kind and sympathetic natures equip them for careers in charity, in catering to the needy, as nurses, as social and health-care workers, or as veterinarians.

Pisces' creativity includes a natural ability to imitate or mirror people as well as empathize with them. These attributes make them wonderful character actors, and many Pisceans find great fulfillment onstage or in films. Pisces are effective in civil service, law enforcement, and the legal and judicial arena.

Details, Details

Pisces is something of a detail-challenged sign—at least this is the perception that many Pisceans have of themselves. They tend to feel that if they fail at the finer points of a project, they won't be able to handle the larger issues. But in point of fact that is not the case. Pisceans have the great gift of intuition, which helps them in all areas of life, but is predominantly helpful at work. This is because they do not always see themselves in the most favorable light in their work and may have to be convinced of their capabilities.

One way Pisceans are good at handling details is the manner in which they use them to illuminate a larger truth. Pisceans are so sensitive and intuitive that even the smallest matters can give them information that very few other people would be able to divine, or even notice at all. Also, although Pisceans may not "file" information in their memories very carefully, they have the ability to ransack their subconscious mind to call up important details when they need them.

Behavior and Abilities at Work

In the workplace, a typical Pisces:

- does not like a strict schedule
- prefers to be behind the scenes
- enjoys work that stimulates creativity
- likes working alone or in a self-directed position
- needs flexibility and frequent change of routine

Pisces As Employer

A typical Pisces boss:

* serves people

* is a creative problem solver

* uses intuition to make decisions

* is a shrewd judge of character

* has a caring disposition

* may use drugs or alcohol

* is charitable and values kindness

* helps staff with personal problems

* may act tough to hide a sensitive nature

Pisces As Employee

A typical Pisces employee:

- is helpful and kind

- has an understanding of the human condition

- needs to exercise her creative imagination

- is sometimes untidy

- may be depressed or moody

- is very affected by negativity

- is a loyal worker when happy

- has good instincts about people

Pisces As Coworker

Pisceans enjoy being in a harmonious workplace and do their part to make the atmosphere pleasant. They have the ability to achieve an overview of any business situation, and their sensitivity enables them to know how others will feel and act. In business, Pisceans work best in creative positions and in public relations, but they may find it hard to do routine jobs or work in groups.

Money

Money is a complicated issue for many Pisceans. They are not materialists in the true sense of the word, and on some level this can work against them. However, when they are in the mood to spend money on the nonessential pleasures of life, they are sometimes guilty of requiring immediate gratification. If they are not careful, this can lead to bad habits that have a negative effect on their life as well as their pocketbook.

Pisceans have an intuitive understanding about nonfinancial resources, and these they handle very well. Falling into this category are friendship, love, the goodwill of those who love them, and even favors that they can depend on the people they love to do, should they be needed. In this way they are extremely capable.

At Home

For a typical Piscean, home is a place where she needs to feel loved. Home can be a palace or a hovel, but it must contain people toward whom she is drawn emotionally and who love her. It is important for Pisces to feel safe and secure in her environment.

Behavior and Abilities at Home

Pisces typically:

* needs a private, personal space

* chooses good food and wine

* likes to escape to the bedroom

* enjoys exploring her imagination

* probably has no fixed routine

* is likely to be untidy

* needs to be surrounded by art and soothing design

* should keep a clock in every room

Leisure
Interests

Pisceans love artistic pursuits and anything that has an element of mystery, fantasy, and imagination. Dangerous sports, such as skydiving or car racing, can also appeal to Pisceans because they have an unerring instinct in such situations. The Piscean love of spirituality is enhanced by nature-related activities such as gardening and taking long walks.

The typical Piscean enjoys the following pastimes:

- theater and films
- stories about witches, monsters, and creatures
- gentle foot massages
- noncompetitive sports
- watercolor classes
- scented bubble baths

Piscean Likes

- 🌸 romantic places

- 🌸 candles and incense

- 🌸 people who need their help

- 🌸 sleeping and dreaming

- 🌸 being loved

- 🌸 reading and writing poetry

- 🌸 yoga and meditation

- 🌸 shoes

- 🌸 mystical gifts and psychics

- 🌸 soft background music

Piscean Dislikes

- harsh, bright lighting
- being sleep deprived
- people knowing too much about them
- stiff or tight clothing
- noisy, crowded places
- dirty jokes
- being told to get a grip on things
- ugly places
- insensitive people
- skeptical attitudes

The Secret Side of Pisces

Sometimes Pisceans desire to escape from experiencing both their own emotions and the emotions of those around them. No one is better than those born under this sign at creating their own fantasy world, through writing and the visual arts, mood-altering substances, or earning enough money to make their world as isolated and comfortable as possible. They get into trouble when they use drugs, alcohol, sex, gambling, religious zealousness, and other escape devices that overwhelm their common sense and block out the real world.

Neptune ♆

Neptune is the planet of transcendent beauty and inspiration. It rules theories about dimensions beyond this one, faith, and the belief in things that cannot be seen, the power of prayer, and the afterlife. When the beauty and idealization of Neptune become clouded by fear, the tendency to want to escape can be as overwhelming as the ocean's currents. This is why Neptune is also associated with drugs, alcohol, and other escapist behavior. It also rules psychic phenomena, when people may actually visit the realms of spiritual power beyond the earthly one. This is the world of intuition, mental telepathy, and extrasensory perception of all kinds.

Neptune rules the feet, and those who learn about the science of reflexology will discover that there are points in the feet that connect to all the other parts of the body.

Bringing Up a Young Pisces

Piscean children absorb information and ideas like a sponge. They should be taught to sort their ideas and to distinguish between what is reality and what is fantasy.

Young Pisceans tend to be vulnerable to friends who might deceive them. Because of their compassionate, passive, and sweet natures, Piscean children may sometimes be the victims of bullies, so it would be useful to teach them strategies for dealing with such situations. An understanding of human nature and some simple, clear rules help young Pisces to avoid those pitfalls—while still developing their valuable traits of love and understanding.

Emotional connections with people are absolutely essential to Piscean happiness. The young Piscean is less concerned with places or things, although they often seek attachments to animals. Consequently, a Pisces child should be helped to believe in herself and prevented from becoming too clingy.

At school, young Pisces usually do not take leadership positions—they prefer to avoid the limelight. However, Piscean children are the source of wonderful ideas for art, play, and adventure. Because they have highly attuned artistic impulses, they should be encouraged to find a channel for their abilities. However, it is a mistake to push them, since their delicate spirit needs to be fostered, not forced.

Pisces As a Parent

The typical Pisces parent:

- encourages the creativity of children

- tends to spoil and overprotect

- may forgive rather than discipline

- listens with understanding

- encourages intuitive development

- may have to try to be punctual

- rarely curses or uses harsh language

- may tend to have an unusual set of rules

- shares fairy tales and magical tales

The Pisces Child

The typical Pisces child:

- loves the world of make-believe
- goes his own way
- has an active imagination
- believes in fairies and angels
- rarely loses his temper
- has a sweet and engaging smile
- has secret conversations with spirits
- is artistically gifted

* loves animals

* looks like something is wrong when lost in thought

* knows how others are feeling

* blurts out things she has no way of knowing—psychic!

* can easily have his feelings hurt

* wants to help those in need

* needs help standing up to bullies

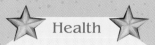

Health

Typical Pisceans are healthy people as long as they are loved. Unhappy Pisceans are vulnerable to alcohol, drugs, or other ways of escaping reality, which is not good for their mental and physical health.

Pisceans can worry, and tend to develop insomnia. If they do relaxing forms of exercise or meditation, they can stay positive. The constant effort of avoiding negativity is the cause of much distress to many Pisceans, who are so intuitive, they often know when someone else is ill and can feel their pain.

Pisceans also need to take care of their feet, which is the part of the body that Pisces rules. They should always wear comfortable shoes.

FAMOUS PISCEANS

Drew Barrymore

Harry Belafonte

Alexander Graham Bell

Johnny Cash

Edgar Cayce

Frederic Chopin

Kurt Cobain

Albert Einstein

Jackie Gleason

Kelsey Grammer

Spike Lee

Jerry Lewis

Eva Longoria

Liza Minnelli

Anaïs Nin

Chuck Norris

Sidney Poitier

Lou Reed

Auguste Renoir

John Steinbeck

Sharon Stone

Elizabeth Taylor

George Washington

Vanessa Williams

Bruce Willis

About the Authors

Internationally known self-help author Monte Farber's inspiring guidance and empathic insights impact everyone he encounters. Amy Zerner's exquisite one-of-a-kind spiritual couture creations and collaged fabric paintings exude her profound intuition and deep connection with archetypal stories and healing energies. Together, they have built The Enchanted World of Amy Zerner and Monte Farber: books, card decks, and

oracles that have helped millions discover their own spiritual paths.

Their best-selling titles include The Chakra Meditation Kit, The Enchanted Tarot, The Instant Tarot Reader, The Psychic Circle, Karma Cards, The Truth Fairy, The Healing Deck, True Love Tarot, Animal Powers Meditation Kit, The Breathe Easy Deck, The Pathfinder Psychic Talking Board, and Gifts of the Goddess Affirmation Cards.

For further information, please visit: **www.TheEnchantedWorld.com**